Blood Magick

Seth

iUniverse, Inc.
New York Lincoln Shanghai

Blood Magick

All Rights Reserved © 2003 by Seth

No part of this book may be reproduced or transmitted in any form or by any means, graphic, electronic, or mechanical, including photocopying, recording, taping, or by any information storage retrieval system, without the written permission of the publisher.

iUniverse, Inc.

For information address:
iUniverse, Inc.
2021 Pine Lake Road, Suite 100
Lincoln, NE 68512
www.iuniverse.com

ISBN: 0-595-29839-7

Printed in the United States of America

Contents

Blood is the Symbol, the Medium, and the Price of Power. vii

Initiation

Threshold 3

The Source 5

The Six Pillars. 7

Application

Sacrifice & Significance. 15

Ritual Magick 18

Symbols of Power 22

Remote Viewing 23

Shapeshifting 25

Grimoire

Blood Amplification 29

Spells 33

Foundation

Medieval Magick 43

vi   Blood Magick

The Flagellant Processions 48
The Little Apocalypse. 53
Omega 56

Blood is the Symbol, the Medium, and the Price of Power.

People will tell you that this book is dangerous. Some will say that blood magick cannot be done, shouldn't be done.

For the weak, ignorant, and gullible these warnings could not be more true.

If you are looking for convenient excuses for violence, unsanitary acts, or excessive self-mutilation, then proceed no further. This book is not for you.

The author of these pages will not be held responsible nor have pity for the misuse of this book or irresponsible deeds done in its name.

This book is about knowledge, transcendence, and power. It has been written for those with the intelligence and forcefulness to seek it.

A note to readers: Words like magick, magic, sorcerer, mage, and many others will be used interchangeably in the chapters that follow. This is done deliberately to expose both the inherent fallacy of language, and the useful illusion of form and versatility that it provides.

Initiation

Threshold

Blood magick is dangerous. The sorcerer uses the power that lies within the physical substance that is blood, with the aim of shaping reality into what he or she wills. This requires enough force to impose one's will upon the world, enough discipline to master the subtleties of arcane lore, and enough willfulness to utilize the potency of blood. A sorcerer who would tap into the power of blood must break free from social and cultural taboos in order to explore the full potential of magick.

Blood magick can be as flashy as one using it to siphon the life energies from others, curse them with disease, or cleanse and heal the self or others. Yet it can be subtle. Reshaping the world requires more than spectacle, it takes time, effort, and transformations of the fundamental patterns that reside deep in the essence of all things. An accomplished sorcerer will understand the appropriate applications of both sorts. Blood magick aims to create a state of mastery over the self and the environment, to remove any barrier between desire and fulfillment.

High blood magic is magic that is enhanced with ritual and the use of blood. By using such essence the sorcerer is able to supercharge the act of ritual, which in turn empowers the spell, which has been brought about like any other spell. So the sorcerer is able to use his or her own maximum energy, the ritual boost, and the power residing with in the blood to exponentially compound the potency of any spell. Spells of this nature are arduous and powerful, allowing those with sufficient discipline, patience, and power to achieve bewilderingly potent results.

Low blood magic is direct magick, the sorcerer's intentions becoming results immediately and with little preparation. An adept might

4   Blood Magick

throw an offensive spell and use an aggressive hand gesture to provide some sympathetic component to her spell. The old adage of "like to like" for example, my blood is your blood. So there is a link between us through our blood, we are both human, so the sympathy is already there, no need for complex rituals the majority of the time. Thinking in this manner makes you able to cast quite effectively on anyone or anything, regardless of shielding or naturally occurring defenses.

Low blood magic, keep in mind that the low\high distinction exists only to differentiate from primarily ritual based and more direct magicks, operates on this sympathy principle. If one looks at unified field theory, or pantheism, or just the idea that all life shares a link and is part of a greater whole, then the connections will be made. In a way, one could call blood magic just a focused form of basic life magic. So a mage could use blood, any blood, to form the sympathetic connection to any other target. Of course the more similar the blood being used is to that of the target the more effective the spell will be.

The Source

In most religions there are paths that believers may take that will, given faith and determination, lead them into a closer relationship with Reality. Sometimes these paths are not at all accepted by the dominant religious tradition, but they exist none the less. These traditions exist because some of the believers in those traditions wanted a more direct experience of Reality, something unmediated by their priests and rulers. From the perspective of those in power this is a most disturbing development. The ability and position of mediation of contact with the divine is the primary reason that such power hierarchies exist.

The mediation of contact with the divine is a way of establishing control. The power to control a person's contact with the divine is the power to control most all aspects of that person's life, future, and perception of the past. These people live under the implied threat of the removal of the divinity in their lives, the loss of wonder and mystery, the loss of hope. The idea that there can be hope without freedom is foolish and blind. Those without freedom are without hope, those without hope are easy to control. The paths that emerged and continue to emerge from the religious traditions of the world are the attempts of a few hearty individuals to throw off the shackles of dogma and meet the Universe on their own terms. Armed with the religious structure of their respective traditions these mystics and seekers of truth band together to make their own way in the world, they establish their own ways of unmediated experience of the divine. In their minds they are still members of their original religious traditions, though they may not be a part of the dogmatic community. They exist on the fringe of their

6   Blood Magick

traditions and cultures. They are respected and feared, loved and hated, always balanced between heresy and innovation.

Many times it has been asked what is to become of those without a tradition? Or those who are already in a religious tradition but find even the fringe communities to be overly dogmatic and in the business of control? The answer is not simple or easy. The path to be set before you is one that should not be taken lightly. Once you begin there is only one way out, and that is to go forward. Always growing. No one can help you, when you walk down this path you do it alone.

One might wonder how magic could be a spiritual path to the divine and not at all be wondering in ignorance. Everything about the modern world tells us that magic does not and cannot exist. We lock up our insane brothers and sisters, we tell ourselves that only science can show us the way of seeing the world. We laugh and heckle the candle peddlers and diviners while we try to convince ourselves that new age hippies are the extent of the community of magic users. We lock away our elders in "resting homes" and wait for them to die instead of listening to their stories and learning their wisdom. We read our history books and religion texts and pretend that the religions of the ancients were founded on superstition and ignorance. Since our childhood we have been force-fed the illusions of our leaders, we have had our imagination and sense of wonder beaten out of us from preschool on. We force our children to see the world the way we do, and never give them the chance to see it the way they do. This is the reason that children can see us for what we are, they are not yet clouded by logic and dogma. We are raised to worship science and reason, and are taught that those who believe in magic cannot believe in science. Science is perhaps one of the most important skills or disciplines one could possess, but it is not the only way of knowing and investigating reality. Science is a tool, and a mage armed with both science and magic is a tremendous force to be reckoned with. Magic, like any other thing that can be seen in its own light, is a viable option for a spiritual path, simply because it exists.

The Six Pillars

There are six pillars that combine to form the system known as Blood Magick. The first four are the primary pillars of Blood, Will, Knowledge, and Unity. These represent the most fundamental elements of all blood magick, and can be found in every aspect of the system.

Blood: The sorcerer seeks to draw upon the inherent potency of blood, more specifically, the magickal essence of blood. Blood in and of itself hold no power, it is merely a nutrient rich fluid that permeates creatures complex enough to have circulatory systems. In its true form, blood magick is drawing upon the magical energy so readily abundant in blood. As the substance that carries the power of life itself; blood is simply the medium. Mere spilt blood has no power, until the sorcerer comes along to unlock the energies within.

It is this potency of blood that forms the entire basis for the tradition. Not only does it both carry and represent power in a physically tangible way, blood is dangerous. Using blood, one's own or that of others, either as a physical magical component or as a basis of visualization and association, tests a sorcerer's limits.

To spill blood as a spell component is violent by necessity, how else but through physical damage can blood be extracted from the body? To use blood as the key symbol or associative focus of a spell, even if none is shed, is considered aberrant thought and behavior by most societies, magical or otherwise. Blood magick, by its very nature, tests social boundaries, breaks taboos, and forces both the sorcerer and those around him or her to come to grips with the potent and immediate reality of magick.

8   Blood Magick

Will: The use of magic is an act of will. Without willpower the magic user cannot use the magic they so fervently believe in. A magic user must be humble enough to understand their place in Reality, and yet be arrogant enough to use their will to shape the fabric of reality as they choose. Willpower is the raw strength of a magic user, the measure of the amount of raw power that the sorcerer is able to bring to bear. The skill of a magic user is defined as the effective use of the will to manipulate reality. This pillar ties all of the four together. The magic user must first believe in magic, then be able to understand the source of magic, then be able to harness that source, and finally be able to willfully shape that force with enough finesse to make it productive.

Knowledge: For this pillar the author will humbly draw upon his own experience, thus providing an overall metaphor and example of practical applications of this pillar.

This is how I made it through high school and college: I had a realization in 11th grade that the seemingly useless subject I was learning, math especially, were only the basic building blocks for higher learning. Then in college, more specifically physics, I learned more about magic in that single class than I had in years of study. Not because I was learning magical rotes and rituals and such, but because I was learning how to see the world through the objective eyes of science.

The more I knew about physical reality the more I was able to discover about magic theory and its application. For example, take senior Biology, I realized then that all I needed to do to really learn potent life magic was to pay attention in class. How can a Life Mage cast any spells of any real importance without knowing about the life systems he or she is dealing with? The more you learn period, the more you learn about magic. In general, the more powerful and knowledgeable mages are also skilled in mathematics, art, language, science, politics, etc.

You can't be a Renaissance Man, or Woman, without education.

Magic is Science is Art is Language.

And the masters of such disciplines are the most potent people the world over. Having power and the will to use it means absolutely noth-

The Six Pillars   9

ing if the sorcerer does not possess the knowledge of it. Knowledge in this case can be defined as a conglomerate product of experience and education.

Unity: In its most basic form, Unity explains that everything has an essence and that this essence is both individual and shared. The second is that all energy is potential magical energy. This principle is taken from the scientific investigations of physicists. Einstein and others have come to the conclusion that all things are energy in some form or another, but that all things are fundamentally energy none the less. If everything is made up a singular existant we call energy, then all things are this singular energy in one form or another.

What follows is the notion that magical energy is this singular energy in a specific form, but since magical energy is this singular energy just the same, then all forms of energy are potentially magical energy. With this principle in mind one can see the infinite power of such a truth. If magic is fueled by magical energy and all energy is potential magical energy then any act of magic is potentially infinitely powerful.

The final pillars are Resonance and Sympathy. It is these two minor pillars that connect with the first, blood, to give this system of magick it's unique potency and permeating flexibility.

Sympathy: "If we analyze the principles of thought on which magic is based, they will probably be found to resolve themselves into two: first, that like produces like, or that an effect resembles its cause; and, second, that things which have once been in contact with each other continue to act on each other at a distance after the physical contact has been severed. The former principle may be called the Law of Similarity, the latter the Law of Contact or Contagion. From the first of these principles, namely the Law of Similarity, the magician infers that he can produce any effect he desires merely by imitating it: from the second he infers that whatever he does to a material object will affect equally the person with whom the object was once in contact, whether it formed part of his body or not. Charms based on the Law of Similar-

10   Blood Magick

ity may be called Homoeopathic or Imitative Magic. Charms based on the Law of Contact or Contagion may be called Contagious Magic. To denote the first of these branches of magic the term Homoeopathic is perhaps preferable, for the alternative term Imitative or Mimetic suggests, if it does not imply, a conscious agent who imitates, thereby limiting the scope of magic too narrowly. For the same principles that the magician applies in the practice of his art are implicitly believed by him to regulate the operations of inanimate nature; in other words, he tacitly assumes that the Laws of Similarity and Contact are of universal application and are not limited to human actions." (Selected excerpt from The Golden Bough, 1922. By Sir James George Frazer)

Resonance: Resonance and the Self-Propagation of Magical Energy When a sorcerer gathers energy to fuel a spell one must remember that the energy is not going to be "pure". It will by all means be pure magical energy, but the energy itself with have what is called a resonance. It is this resonance, or flavor if you will, of the energy that will determine some of its unique qualities.

For example, if a wizard happens upon a burial ground and finds it necessary for whatever reason to cast a spell, the energy that he gathers will have the flavor of those burial grounds. Perhaps this visualization, magical energy could easily be seen metaphorically as water. Water is water, but water from any source will be different on some level than water from another source. There is distilled water, pond water, river water, ocean water, sewage, run off, and precipitation. Water tends to take on characteristics of its environment, so it is with magical energy. It is for this reason that a witch from a rural area might find that her spell feels different when powered by magical energy from a city than from her home ground.

Resonance tends to self-propagate. For example, the energy of a city powers wizards in its area of influence, and those wizards continue to use its power. Like the magical muscles of spellcasting, so to it is with locations of power. The more they are tapped for energy, as long as they are not burned out, they grow back stronger. Now perhaps it is more clear just how powerful the spreading of cities really is, because as all magic users know, normal people can be affected by the energy of a location just as easily as mages or spirits.

Not only does the location of the magical energy effect the resonance of the energy, the resonance of the energy directly effects the spellcaster himself. Think of the old cliché "you are what you eat". This very much applies to magic users in two major ways. The first is that magic users are more affected by the resonance of locations than normal people, and sustained exposure to such locations affect magic users just like it does the magical energy in its area of influence. So the more attuned to a location, or certain type of energy (nature, urban, death, etc) a magic user is, the more it will "color" their spells. More often than not magic users are easily identified by what sort of magic they seem to be doing, the resonance of their energy.

It is this coloring of the spells by the resonance of the magical energy that is the second way in which the resonance directly affects the magic user herself. Think of the metaphor of the athlete. If a person trains constantly for running, they will develop the long and lean body type of a runner. If a person is a weight lifter or football player, they will develop the stocky body type that best fits their chosen sports. All sports are like this to some degree, with a certain body type being superior to all others in that particular sport. Now, what would happen to a runner who tried to enter a bodybuilding contest? Or a ballerina who suddenly had to play football?

This is what happens to magic users who allow themselves, for better or worse, to take on the resonance of a specific type of magical energy. The more healing spells a person casts, the more permeated with the healing resonance they become. The result is that they become an immaculate healer, but their abilities in say death magic or astral projection might very well suffer. While it tends to be natural for magic users to become permeated to at least a moderate degree with one sort of magical energy resonance, it can become detrimental to the flexibility of the seeker sort of magic user to become trapped in one of these aspects. For example, a blood mage is incredibly powerful when he has access to the fluids he requires. Deny him those components or energy patterns, and he will be in serious jeopardy, unless another solution presents itself. Though such a lack is highly unlikely given that the sorcerer almost always has access to his own body.

Energy resonance can be garnered just about anywhere and doing any sort of magic. It is no different for a wandering wizard. As a traveler the wandering wizard will have the ability to maintain a relatively clean slate when it comes to resonance from locations. Also, with a clear mind and a taste for variety the wanderer will be able to avoid a spell type rut. Yet one must accept the fact that the wandering wizard over time becomes permeated by the energy of motion. So travelers should take care that they stop sometimes. As said above, resonance permeation can make one incredibly powerful, but limits the magic user who is trapped in that aspect. One must be aware that overmuch avoidance of at least a moderate amount of permeation will lead to resonance of "jack of all trades, master of none", which can also limit one's progress. So in conclusion, be aware of your permeation levels. They are both a strength and a weakness.

Application

Sacrifice & Significance

Blood is the connective element, both figuratively and literally that allows the blood sorcerer to tightly focus spells upon their target, adapt without difficulty, and always have a magical "angle of approach". The fact that this angle can be found in either the physicality of blood rites or the associations of energy is what gives this system a great deal of its power.

Blood, when used as the crux of a magical paradigm, becomes a renewable resource. The proper harvesting and usage of this substance is crucial. Mindless carnage robs blood of its potency by devaluing its significance. Obsessive application of self-mutilation replaces the deeper meanings of blood with the frantic instability of mental illness. Carelessness with the blood of others puts the sorcerer at risk for poisoning and disease. There are many dangers in blood magick, these are but a few. The sorcerer must be mindful of the source of the blood, maintain awareness of its potency, and keep vigilant against being distracted by the spilling of it.

It is possible that during one's career as a blood sorcerer there may come a time when sacrifice is necessary. Always remember that the sacrifice of a living being is nothing short of murder. If you pursue this course of action understand that responsibility must be taken, accept that the sacrifice is a murder, even if a necessary one. To believe any other way is to invite excessive callousness and a disconnection from the inherent power of blood, not to mention that sacrifice is illegal in the eyes of most temporal governments.

16   Blood Magick

There are many ways in which to gather shed blood, what follows are a few guidelines to aid the aspirant in developing a personal framework for the harvesting of it.

The first, and most common, is the act of cutting. The most potent choice would be to perform the cutting upon oneself, thus benefiting from the clarity that controlled pain can often bring. Also, the blood of a sorcerer who is actually involved in the casting of the spell has much more potency and significance than any other blood source. Though blood is blood, so any source will serve the sorcerer's purpose.

It is suggested that the cutting instrument be as sharp as possible, like a scalpel or razor, so as to prevent excessive scarring. Though scars can be used to store power or as magical focusing tools, much like any tattoo or body paint, it is best not to cause a scar when the only intention of the cutting is to draw blood. If one intends to draw blood, then do so, only scar when the scar is the desired product of the act.

The forearms, thighs, and biceps are the most efficient locations for extraction via cutting. These areas of the body bleed well when wounded, but do not incapacitate or cause mortal danger to the recipient should the cuts be made too deep. The chest is a good location when a more potent source is needed, as is the abdomen. Though great care must be taken for these areas, cutting too deeply into the chest or abdomen can cause severe damage and possibly death. The lips are more sensitive, requiring a more skilled application of the blade, but yield potent blood, given the symbolic connection most humans make with the soul and the face.

The second method of blood harvesting is the use of the needle. While the act of cutting provides a more dramatic, dangerous, and ultimately more potent magical result, a discerning sorcerer would do well to develop skill with the needle. Using a needle to draw blood is far less invasive, requires less skill, and produces just as much blood for the effort. The benefit of pain is not as present in this technique, but it is far more discreet and easily hidden from outsiders. A gash on one's forearm is much more difficult to hide or explain than a pinpricked fingertip concealed by a band-aid.

The most effective harvest points are the lips and fingertips. Both areas bleed profusely when wounded, and are quick to heal, depending upon the size of the needle. If a large sieve-like needle, such as those used for donating blood, are used, then one must be very cautious. Puncture wounds take time to heal and the blood flow from such wounds can be difficult to stop. Thus, it is recommended that smaller needles be used, once again pointing out that the act of drawing blood must lend itself to the act of magic, not supercede it.

Also, always have the proper medical supplies present should any significant bloodletting be desired.

Ritual Magick

As human beings we are creatures of images. In our earliest times to the present we have been enamored of images. We make paintings on cave walls and carvings or statues of our gods and heroes. As we have expanded our range of mediums of imagery we seem to have become much more reliant upon external imagery than a translation of the internal to the external. In essence, we have lost or suppressed that inner imagery for favor of the easier and less committed imagery of the external. Instead of listening to storytellers and dancing out our myths we watch movies and play high-tech video games. It isn't that these more modern mediums of image expression are better or worse than those of the past, the problem is that these modern mediums have become so central that the old ways have been all but ousted. While the modern mediums are wonderful and deeply expressive and rich in visual qualities, they lack the deep internal commitment that dancing and storytelling demand. In many ways we have pushed away our ability to visualize and express for ourselves internally, we have to have something tangible, like a movie or a book. For the magic user visualization is not only a necessary talent, but also a cultivated skill.

Any action executed by a human being requires visualization on the part of the person. Even something as simple as reaching for a glass of water. The person visualizes a glass of water in their hand and so doing, reaches for the glass and picks it up. The same basic principle is at work in any act of magic. Once a mage has reached the point where they have ascended and no longer need visualization beyond the basics, executing a magical act is no more complicated than moving one's arm to

Ritual Magick 19

collect a glass of water. However, for those of us who are not at that step a more complicated process of visualization is necessary.

When a mage casts there must be an internal visualization of what is going on around and inside them. Because magic is normally an act whose effects and results tend to exist in the realm of the invisible the mage must visualize both its process and results. This visualization shapes the spell and empowers it. Without any shame or reservation the mage must see internally through the imagination the channeling of the power, the shaping of it, and the casting of it. For many this may be a sufficient amount of visualization, because their imaginations are vivid enough that they are able to create enough of a personally believable visualization that they cast the spell without many external clues as to what they are doing.

For many others however, simply visualizing the spell's creation and use just isn't sufficient. This is the role of ritual in magic. A ritual is any external process executed for the purpose of casting a spell or producing some supernatural effect. Rituals can be as simple as lighting a candle or as complicated as month long purifications or choreographed movements and special words. The purpose of all ritual is to focus the participant's attention and power to a fine point. Ritual also provides a potent structure and shape for the energies being used by the participants. Here is an example: The reason blood and bones are such important parts of magic are that they are very powerful conductors and receptacles of energy. Partly because of their relationships to the physiology of life. Blood carries life, bones support it. Also, due to our perception of those relationships we are more open in our hearts and minds to the fact that these items can be used in magic. Many times these items are more powerful than many other things, as long as we believe and make them so. Bones and blood can be used in magic not related to the animal itself, or even a use that doesn't deal directly with life. It is a way of making the invisible world of magic seemingly tangible long enough to create a space in which the two worlds meet and powerful magics can be wrought.

This leads again to the idea of high and low magic. First let it be said that all magic is equal in that it is shaped energy, there may be a degree of separation in that one spell may be more powerful than another, but they are equal in their potential power and thus fundamentally the same. The idea of high and low magic is an illusion, sometimes necessary for those who choose to use it as a paradigm for their magical workings. High magic is magic that requires ritual in order to perform and tends to have very potent effects. Low magic is magic that requires little to no ritual and while at times potent, tends to be less invasive. In this system low magic is magic that requires no ritual on the part of the mage, and provides room for growth in that greater magic has the potential to be lesser magic once the mage has gained enough control over the energy.

This is an example of the self-imposed paradigms that dominate the realm of magic. While magic itself is totally without moral and dogmatic limitations, those who practice magic are. This is because we are human beings and have a compulsion towards structure and order. This is why there are so many different paths of magic, "schools" if you will. There are shamans, witches, diviners, and necromancers just to name a few. All of which have their own styles of magic and rules to govern them. For example, in medieval necromancy there was an emphasis on the study of magical tomes and grimoires before an adept even made the attempt to undertake a magical working. Another example is the more modern versions of witchcraft, which insists on the illusion that all magic comes back on the caster threefold. These are all paradigms that would not exist if no one believed in them. Much like the laws of physics. If we as a society chose to deny the existence of gravity as a mass relationship and defined it as some greedy god pulling everything towards it, we could not be proven wrong, just as those who believe in gravity cannot be proven wrong.

We define magic, like gravity and physics, by its relationships because those relationships are the only reasons that we are able to perceive its existence. Since those relationships are a multitude, the inter-

Ritual Magick 21

pretations of those relationships will exist in a multitude. Basically the belief system that one ascribes to is the one that they use to live in a defined reality, they know exactly what they are capable of and live accordingly. Someone without a permanent paradigm walks a much harder path in that they live in a world of mystery and the unknown, but for these people the potential for growth is much more. Metaphorically, the believer is a warrior who only trains with one weapon, and so becomes a master so long as it is with that particular weapon. The person with no set paradigm is the warrior who is familiar with all weapons but is not a master of any one in particular, and so is never unarmed. I have always believed that a person on the path of the mage should treat paradigms like clothing. If it is hot, wear a t-shirt and shorts. If it is cold, wear pants and a coat. The same goes for rituals. If the situation is such that the mage wants a boost in focus and power, a ritual can be done. Or if there is something the mage wants to accomplish right away a spell can just be cast without any structured elements. The beauty of blood magick is that it has the power to transcend paradigms. Wiccans, Thelemites, Chaos Mages, Clerics, or any manner of magic user can utilize blood magick. Like gravity, blood connects us all, regardless of our belief systems or magical approaches to its use.

Symbols of Power

Almost every magical tradition worldwide has a physical element to their magical practices. The practice of using physical representation of the magic to be cast and the desired result is generally called sympathetic magic. Runes and effigies and other symbols of power are a product of such practices. Effigies are actually physical representations of people, places, or things that are the focus of spells. Two examples of this would be a vodoun sorcerer making a doll out of cloth and using the hair and semblance of the recipient of the blessing or the curse. Another would be an Egyptian sorcerer making wax boats, putting them in a bowl of water and shaking the bowl, causing an invading fleet to sink beneath unusually large waves.

Runes are similar. They are symbols and patterns that allow the caster to focus on a certain element of reality. This flexibility of symbolic representation is the reason why there are so many rune systems throughout the world. This is the reason that I say each mage, while keeping the others in mind, should always search for other symbols and patterns that channel the energy of creation. It is like language, the more words known the more versatile and specific sentences can be formed. One can also "discover" or "invent" previously unused runes and symbols. One merely has to become attuned and aware enough to notice them as they come along.

Remote Viewing

There is a growing perceived need in the global community for more hi-tech intelligence gathering and analyzing methods and equipment. Computer technology, satellites, code machines and a myriad of other devices and contraptions serve the intelligence agencies of the modern era. I believe that the use of locators may become more commonplace as the infallibility and cost of technology rises. Remote Viewing is a practical and tangible application of psychic or magical energy to the task of locating or perceiving a person or place without being physically present. Remote Viewing was used by the Central Intelligence Agency in the 70's and 80's, but was allegedly discontinued for inaccuracy and inconsistency. Remote Viewing is like all other abilities and powers of the mind and spirit, it is unpredictable and not infallible. A remote viewer may see the layout of an enemy fortress accurately one day, and then fail to do so the next with a different base. That doesn't change the fact that it was done the first time.

Remote Viewing can be accomplished in one of several ways. One possible method is to go into a meditative trance with a map of the world, region, or area in question at one's fingertips. If the target is a person then perhaps the locator has an item connected to that person, or has become familiar with faces and sensitive information about that person. If the target is a location like a building, then personal effects won't matter. With the fingertips held slightly above the map the locator will move them all over the map until a ripple in the psyche or the mind occurs, a change in the energy of the map. It is this point of flux that the locator is on watch for, there is where the target will be. If the details of the building or area are needed the locator allows the subconscious image to surface in the mind.

Another method of remote viewing is via astral projection, or known to some as spiritwalking. The locator goes into a meditative state and uses astral projection or spiritwalking to push their consciousness into the outer world. From there the same mapping method is employed. However, the locator is navigating with an instinctual map, a global awareness that cannot fit on a page. Once this global connection is made the locator goes on intuition in order to find the target. Like the previous method, the more facts known prior to the session is best, perhaps the first method would serve best as a preparation for the second. In the astral realm or spiritworld the locator can find the target and report back with much more firsthand detail than if no contact was made.

Shapeshifting

Depending upon what cultural approach you take, your answer is determined. It is a common practice in most cultures of the world. There are several theories on the art of shapeshifting and so several varieties of shapeshifting. The first discussed will be the physical act of shapeshifting. This is a case in which the user shifts around the physiology of the body to suit the needs of the user. Examples of this would be a man turning into a cheetah so that he might run quickly, or a wolf so that he might be stronger. This sort of shapeshifting is quite rare, and usually out of reach for most adepts who are not focused upon that goal. This is usually something achievable only by shamanic masters and spirits or creatures like the doppelganger.

The second sort of shapeshifting is much more common. It is when a person or thing changes an aspect of themselves in order to gain certain advantages. An example would be a person taking on the senses of a wolf, the strength of a bear, or the underwater breathing of a fish. It could be something as mundane as growing claws to developing the benefits different respiration organs. One might ask if the observer could see such changes. The answer would be yes. Would the changes be overtly physical in actuality? Usually the answer would be no. It is a shaping of energy into a specific form and function, and like most magic, remains mostly unseen. The third kind of shapeshifting is the changing of the avatar, the spirit-self. Much like the first physical shapeshifting, yet upon the spirit or astral plane. Which, like all things in such a place, affects to some degree the physical plane. Giving the user some elements of the first two methods. For any of the shapeshifting methods, adding portions of blood from the creature one wishes to

26   Blood Magick

shift into will speed up the process and increase the totality of the change.

Grimoire

Blood Amplification

The amplifiers are one of the main things that makes blood magick so different from any other system of magick. Fundamentally the amplifiers are magical constructs of blood that increase the energy output of the sorcerer using them. A possible metaphor for the amps would be that each amp is a personally significant rune or sigil inscribed in blood upon the aura of the sorcerer. The sorcerer meditates in order to establish a stable visualization of his or her own aura or spell sphere, and grafts the amp to it. Whatever ritualization the sorcerer feels is personally relevant will increase the amp's potency. The ritual could be as complex as drawing sigils in blood upon the sorcerer himself, or as elaborate as the spilling of large quantities of blood as a ritual sacrifice in exchange for power. So when the sorcerer pushes energy outwards through a spell, the spell passes through the amplifier, unlocking the power of the blood that makes up the amp, and its power is increased.

An imaginary numbering system, which begins with 1 and has the potential to increase ad infinitum, has been developed to illustrate and explain amplifiers. In essence these numbers and notations mean nothing, but they are convenient illusions that will aid in the teaching and defining of the blood amplifiers. Each amplifier has a designation such as B1. Each generation of amplifier is based on the relative power of the sorcerer that creates it, thus as the sorcerer grows in power new generations of blood amps must be created. That makes every amp different from any other amplifier, which is why it gets another B number. Each successive amp in the below list, normally increases one's power exponentially over the previous one, though for each individual the increase

30   Blood Magick

may differ. Once again, the numbers below are imaginary and relative to the individual sorcerer who possesses the amp.

B1—This simply provides +5 to +12 power. This is common in other magical systems, and might be referred to as a focus rune/spell.
B2 x3 power
B3 x10 power
B4 x100 power
And so on towards power unimagined...

In operation, according to the theoretical model above, they give you an effective ability of movement of power times your base level. In essence, the ability to channel more raw power into a spell. For example, a sorcerer with a personal power of 24 using a properly powered B2, would cast spells at 72 power. Though the sorcerer is still a 24 power being, the magical output that the sorcerer is capable of is significantly increased.

The main difference between the B2, B3 and B4 application is that each can only efficiently use so much power before it can't use any more power to apply to the amplification process. This is because as a sorcerer grows in power over time, the amps will cease to be advantageous. For example, once the sorcerer at 24 power gains enough skill, focus, and power, he will be able to craft a much more potent amp for himself. Thus the sorcerer discards the B2 and creates a B3 because he is now able to do so. These amplifiers only scale your power, it really doesn't give you greater detail control within that larger power. This is why a sorcerer cannot simply go from a B1 to a B4 over night, it takes time, patience, and discipline.

However, the benefits of even the smallest amp are beyond measure. Because these amps are permanent constructs, they remain active unless the sorcerer chooses to power them down for a time. Once again, visualizing the amps as runes or sigils of blood that have been etched or grafted to the sorcerer's aura is useful indeed. The casting

Blood Amplification 31

ability increases, simply because you can put more power behind things (so your shields are bigger, your will against other spells and such is greater, your spells are exponentially more potent, etc.).

At their most basic level, blood amps are external modifications of the sorcerer's aura. When the sorcerer casts a spell it must pass through the aura, or spell sphere, on it's way towards the target. It is during this passage that the amp further multiplies the power of the spell. In many ways, amps could be seen as magical rail guns, charging up the already powerful spell projectile and sending it on it's way. However, regardless of how powerful the amps become, their power output depends totally on what power the sorcerer is able to put in, and thus are limited by the sorcerer's own personal power. This is where the IBAs come in.

Internal Blood Amps function the same way as the external blood amps, though they are internal. These amps are grafted to the actual soul/avatar of the sorcerer. Once you start to play with the workings of one's own soul, your base power starts to increase on it's own. The IBAs actually go inside the soul to take the raw energy residing in blood in order to amplify the base personal power levels of the sorcerer. The process of their creation is the same as the externals, though it must be done with a significant amount of focus, self-awareness, and skill. The sorcerer hoping to accomplish this feat must be a master of meditation, biofeedback, and the creation of external amps.

IB1 (otherwise known as InternalB1) is the combination of the techniques of B1 and the modification of the inner soul/avatar of the sorcerer. IBAs are a transformation of one's own soul. To transforms one's own soul requires as much power as can be mastered, thus knowledge and use of powerful external blood amps is a prerequisite. As far as the numerical model, the IBAs provide power amplification at the same ratio as the external blood amps.

So combined with the external amps, the sorcerer is powerful beyond what is possible in most other traditions. For example, a sorcerer with personal power 50 creates a B2. Now her spells are cast at power 150. Then she successfully grafts an IBA2 to her soul/avatar, and is able to transfigure her inner self to use the IBA2. Her personal power remains at a 50, but when she wants to cast a spell she has a personal power output of 150. Then her spell goes through the B2, making her spells cast at 450. Thus, if she were of any other non-blood tradition, her spells would only be as powerful as her personal power. Through blood she is powerful beyond measure.

Spells

This spellbook is a collection of spells and magical workings. While the origins and the stories of the discoveries of many of these spells are far too numerous to tell, you the reader have a unique opportunity to reap the rewards of those adventures and hours of study. Within this work you will find spells that enable the magic user to accomplish feats unimagined, but also the much simpler spells not commonly thought of. That is the purpose of this book, to open the mind of the reader to the endless possibilities of blood magick, regardless of tradition or creed. This is the teaching of the fundamentals of spellcraft by example. What is done with the magic, be it of good or evil, is up to the reader.

Each spell is listed by an appropriately descriptive name and possible situations in which they could be used. The two realms in which these spells are meant to function are the astral and the physical. The astral realm is the general term for realms beyond the ken of physical reality. Places such as the spiritworld, dreamscapes, or ethereal cyberspace. The physical realm is the world of facts and science, the world in which action and reaction are somewhat predictable. An advantage of predictable outcomes at the disadvantage of less spectacular magical results.

After the realm of affects has been defined the method and effects of the spell are clearly defined. Most descriptions will refer to various patterns. These patterns are basic elements of reality that are utilized, conjured, and altered in order to shape and focus spells. These patterns are such things as matter patterns, life patterns, and elemental patterns to name a few. They are felt and manipulated by the user's magical senses and magical will respectively. The magical senses are the extraordinary

34   Blood Magick

senses of magic user's that allow them to become intimately aware of their environment as well as objects and entities within that environment. The magical will is the internal force of change wielded by the magic user to take control of or manipulate magical energy and accomplish the magical feat. While ritual and material components are not vital to any spell, they greatly increase the potency of the spell and the focus of the magic user, and so are useful elements in any spell.

While this book is exhaustive not every possible spell is listed here, there are an infinite number at your fingertips. Let this simply be a stepping-stone into a larger world.

Basic Spells: One simple method of making any magick a part of the blood magick system is to spill your blood or that of another prior to the casting. Thinking of blood as a magical ingredient for any spell greatly increases the versatility of the ways in which it can serve you. Smear it on blades, draw runes with it, anoint oneself or others during a ritual. The possibilities are endless because the blood itself forges an instant and near unbreakable bond between target and caster, a magical circuit through which the spell can flow. What follows are a few spells designed to provide a glimpse into the world of blood sorcery, they are examples only and by no means the totality of the system.

Insight: The sorcerer is able to take a biomatter sample from any living or once living being, and glean information about its source. The sorcerer focuses his will upon the sample, using the bonds of blood to form a magical circuit. While in this state of intense scrutiny the sorcerer, depending upon the potency of his magick, can learn anything from what sort of being the sample came from, its gender, emotions, strengths, weaknesses, just to name a few.

(Components) The more pre-Insight knowledge the sorcerer has of the target the better. Most blood sorcerers will find that merely holding the sample will allow them to do their work, some may need to use meditations, scientific instruments, or perhaps even actual consumption of the sample in order to gain Insight.

Spells 35

Biofeedback: This is a meditative exercise in which the sorcerer is able to achieve total awareness and control of her bodily functions. By visualizing the consciousness as flowing through the body alongside one's own blood, this total awareness can be achieved. Damaged areas can be investigated, diseases fought, nutrients redistributed, organs repaired, the possibilities are limited only by the knowledge and ability of the sorceress herself.

(Components) While most sorcerers are able to achieve at least a basic state of biofeedback with only meditation some may find it useful to concentrate on the inner bloodflow as a focal point.

The Walls Have Eyes: This spell instills a basic awareness within the home of the caster. Walls, mirrors, tables, hangings, and all manner of baubles and household clutter can be made to observe the goings on within the home. The sorcerer can then use his power to retrieve the observations of these items. Walls could speak of intruders, chairs may tell who last sat upon them, mirrors show who last looked through them. Depending upon the potency of the sorcerer and types of information sought the items may show images, impressions, emotions, or magical vibrations.

(Components) The caster simply needs to carefully spread one drop of blood discreetly upon each item he wishes to bestow the powers of observation. Then, when he chooses to investigate the object's findings, the sorcerer will call upon the bonds of blood to form a connection with the object to witness its observations.

Scry: This is a divination spell that allows the caster to pour over the threads of fate directly tied to him. By focusing the will upon the medium the sorcerer is able to pick up on imminent events, pertinent feelings, and impressions of the ripples in reality caused by future events coming his way.

(Components) Simply fill a basin with water, spill the caster's own blood into the vessel. Seek the divination in the swirls and clouds made by the diluting blood.

Consume: This spell allows the caster to steal away the life energies of anyone that the caster comes in flesh-to-flesh contact with. The caster creates a physical sympathetic component for the connection via the bond of blood. Through the circuit the caster drains away the energy within the target, taking it into himself, making him temporarily more powerful or filling him should he be low on energy.
(Components) The most effective ritual component is a thorn, hollow needle, or some other symbolically penetrating object soaked in blood that is carried concealed upon the caster's person. The amount of power taken, rate of drain, and the target's awareness of the drain are all dependent upon the power and skill of the caster.

Forging a Link: This spell allows the sorcerer or sorcerers to share the magical energy reserves of another person or group of people. The caster soaks a number of small stones in blood. The number of stones depends upon how many people are taking part in the power sharing. The blood is most effective if it comes from the participants, though blood from another source is still sufficiently potent to work. Each person taking part in the power network places a soaked stone underneath their tongue. As long as they hold the stone they and those also possessing stones can draw freely upon the power of everyone in the network.
(Components) Each stone should be small enough to be held firmly and comfortably under the tongue. This spell is quite effective should one sorcerer need to draw upon the power of many, or this can form incredible power solidarity within a group.

The Evil Eye: Known throughout time as on of the most powerful of curses. This spell is the fundamental sending from which all other curses find their root. It is the magical manifestation of hatred, malice, ill will, and the wish to cause harm upon another. The sorcerer summons up all such feelings, focusing the will so intently that the negative energy, the desire to curse, becomes manifest. The potency of the curse depends upon the sorcerer and the degree to which he wishes to harm his target. The degree of harm that can be manifested is limited by the power and skill of the sorcerer. The curse could be simply a stigma, where social interactions become difficult. Or it could be a curse of moderate severity, a minor sickness or lasting injury, the target becoming a social outcast. The most potent curses, those that only the most powerful of sorcerers can perform, can cause wasting diseases, permanently cripple, bestow life threatening bad luck, or even go so far as to put the target immediately into harm's way.

(**Components**) For most minor to moderate curses hand gestures and harsh words suffice to deliver the curse through the circuit created by the bonds of blood. For more horrific curses the sorcerer may find that some ritual sacrifice of blood or sympathetic representation, like a statue or a doll ritually harmed, may be necessary to fully lay the curse.

Cleanse: This spell allows the caster to extract and dispose of all manner of detritus, both physical and magical. By focusing the will during an intense ritual cleaning, the sorcerer can divest herself of any enchantments laid upon her, astral parasites, negative energies, troublesome emotions, physical maladies, and mundane uncleanliness. The power of the caster determines the degree of cleanliness that one can reach, for there are many spells that do not dissipate so easily or parasites that let go without a fight.

(**Components**) The most effective manner of casting this spell is in the form of a ritual bath. Draw a bath of water while mixing in three drops of the caster's own blood. This infuses the bath with the sorcerer's power and desire to extract detritus of both physical and spiritual nature. The blood bath will also serve to trap the detritus once the caster leaves. Allowing the caster to safely investigate or dispose of unwanted spells, grime, or astral hangers on. The caster must remem-

38   Blood Magick

ber however that such a deep cleaning will remove positive spells and symbiotes as well unless attention is spent upon maintaining them throughout the ritual.

Accelerate Metabolism: This spell is designed to give the caster the power to accelerate the metabolism of one target, be it the caster himself or another target life form. The caster focuses upon the metabolic centers within the body and uses the will to artificially stimulate these areas. This spell increases the natural rate of metabolism in the body of the target. This increases the healing abilities of the body but also increases the need for food and sleep. This spell is useful for rapid recuperation or can be used in a passive aggressive offensive manner to "thin" opponents over time. This spell does not apply in the astral in most cases, as physiology is more fluid in that realm.
(Components) Knowledge of the physical body of the target's species is a tremendous aid for the visualization of the metabolic centers. Usually a laying of hands upon the target works best. Though if the spell is being cast upon oneself then a piece of straw or incense lit at both ends and anointed with blood can aid the caster in visualizing the spell.

Spitting Blood: For this dramatic and potent spell the caster infuses a physical substance with corrosive energy patterns and hurls the substance at a target. The enchanted substance will behave differently depending upon what realm the spell was cast in. In the astral the substance works like a strong acid, eating away at any material that it touches. In the physical the substance, aside from shocking and surprising the target, will corrode through magical shields to damage the body's energy fields and harm the spirit.
(Components) The most effective component is blood, though in a pinch water or spittle will suffice. Remember that the substance is merely the vehicle for the corrosive energy patterns, but a substance that is reminiscent of fluid works best.

Spells 39

Adventure's Call: This divination spell allows the caster to put himself into a state of heightened awareness and attunement to potential adventures as he comes into contact with them. As most people walk through life they live it reactively, the only adventure that comes into their lives is when such things cross their paths. This spell is designed to give the caster sufficient awareness to notice potential adventures as he goes through his life. The caster will walk down the street and feel a pull towards a back alley. One could be walking in the wood and feel the urge to take a different path than planned. There are infinite possibilities and limitless adventures that people pass up everyday simply because they don't notice them. By going into a meditative state the caster focuses his will upon his own perceptions and creates a magical energy field about himself that is sensitive to and amplifies the subtle irregular patterns in reality. These irregularities are the adventures in their potential forms. Magic users who often employ this spell are constantly involved in some sort of goings on, and seem to be on top of things as they happen.

(Components) This spell is a complex one, and the components are much more personalized. To create and maintain this energy field with mind and will alone is a difficult task, as such most magic users who use this spell utilize talismans or other fetishes, bonded to them through the connection of blood to maintain the energy field once it has been erected. Any sort of personally significant object that can be used as the focal point and source of the field will do.

Old Wounds: This spell allows the caster to cause further harm to a target who suffers from preexisting wounds or to reopen older healed wounds. By extending the senses into the target the caster can become aware of the life pattern of the target, as well as the irregularities in the pattern that represent the wounds. The caster then exerts his will upon the irregularities and imbues them with power, increasing their prominence within the pattern. This spell causes old wounds to reopen, small cuts to bleed profusely, and burns to turn out to be much more severe in addition to many other form of increased trauma. As with many spells, the intensity of the agitation depends directly upon the skill and power of the caster. Also, the effects will be much more spectacular in the astral, though the effects in the physical are no less potent.

(Components) Physically touching the target is the most helpful and effective component, though verbal components such as indications of the increasing pain are also effective. Sympathetic representations of the target, with the wounds visibly recreated, can provide an excellent ritual connection through which to strike.

Foundation

Medieval Magick

Many people, if asked, would agree with the assertion that the modern western view of reality is somewhat narrow. We see what our five senses can perceive. We live in a world dominated by hard science and logic. If something cannot be empirically supported, it is not held to be true. We refuse to accept paradoxes. We strive to find homogeneity in the world around us. We experiment, rationalize, and categorize in an attempt to solve the mystery of our existence. For us, there is no reality outside that which can be defined using our current level of scientific scrutiny.

How did our vision of the world become so narrow? In order to discover the answer we must go back to the last period of western history in which people did not live with such a narrow view of the world. This period is commonly referred to as the Middle Ages. The Medieval period was the twilight of a commonly held view of reality that went deeper than the five senses.

The medieval mind saw a world that was full of possibilities, some of which were wondrous, and others most terrifying. It was a world full of ghosts, spirits, monsters, and magic. It was the belief in magic that made their view of reality so expansive. It is this belief that allowed them to entertain serious ideas about ghosts, monsters, and other seemingly fantastical phenomenon. The medieval mind had no problem living with paradoxes. Thus, magic makes the impossible possible, and perceived reality becomes a realm of unfathomable possibilities.

The majority of the rural population of the medieval period was somehow involved in the practice of magic, by direct involvement or by the belief in its existence. Despite the fact that Christianity was the official religion and that most rural people were baptized or converted, almost all people still adhered in various degrees to pagan beliefs and practices. It was common for peasants of that time to be only nominally Christian and remain a pagan in practice. Their lack of dissonance over this issue further illustrates the general acceptance of paradox in the medieval mindset.

Magic, for the scope of this section, will be considered any action or attempt that is made to affect a change in reality by any means that is not considered "ordinary". The use of plant material by itself would not be magic, but using these materials in conjunction with mystical words or rituals would be magic. In the medieval mind words carried a certain potency, and the use of words and phrases as magic was common amongst the magic-users of the time. Rituals, dances, songs, trances, and any other extraordinary activities could be considered magical. Also, some types of healing among the peasants were considered magic by those involved.

At its most basic level, magic is control, the ability to influence one's situation through extraordinary means. This is the reason the peasants held on so fiercely to the practice of magic, sometimes suffering penance for magical acts that they felt important enough to suffer for. In a world as mysterious and frightening as theirs, stability and security were major issues. The practice of magic gave the peasants and opportunity to take control of their own lives in a world where they had little control over anything.

There are two basic types of control offered by magic. The first is control of the person. This sort of control is embodied in the magic that affects people directly. Healing magic is the most obvious, when the magic-user utilizes certain plant and animal materials in conjunction with gestures and spoken words in order to heal a wounded or sick person. Another example would be a curse, in which the magic user would cause bad things to happen directly to the victim of the curse. The second type of control offered by magic is the control of nature. This sort of control is embodied in the magic that directly affects things in nature. An example of this type of control would be the use of magic to affect weather patterns. The use of magic to directly affect crops and livestock is another example. With magic the peasants were able to control the environment in which they lived. They could heal the sick, stop droughts, and bring fertility to their crops and livestock.

In addition to control, magic also possessed another important feature; it allowed for unmediated contact with the divine. Many of the magical workings of the peasants called upon the forces of nature, the power of the person, and the grace of God. The belief in magic was an important factor in the deep view of reality held by the peasants. In this world of infinite possibilities and mysteries, the potential for direct experience of God was great indeed. With this view of reality, and the ability to experience God directly, there was not a total reliance upon the Church for mediation of contact with God.

The belief in magic itself did not seem to bother the Church as much as the result of the belief and the actual practice of it. The Church never denied the existence and potency of magic, but it condemned it none the less. According to the Church the practice of magic was an act of pagan heresy, and that the only magic that was not diablerie was that of the Church's saints. Even then, the Church did not consider the actions of the saints to be magical. The Church viewed what the saints did as supernatural but not necessarily magical. Their power was coming from God, the source of the supernatural. An example of this would be exorcism, while such an act was not officially considered by the Church to be magic; it does fit the definition of magic.

The saints of the medieval period were known for their prowess in the performance of miracles. The Church did not consider these miracles diablerie because the power of the saints allegedly came directly from God. The problem with saints was in proving that they were empowered by God instead of being cleverly disguised sorcerers. Most of those saints who were acknowledged as such were members of the Church hierarchy already, and had no need to convince anyone of their source of power. Saints who were not already connected with, and thus controlled by the Church, were shunned and sometimes imprisoned or killed. Because they were independent, they were forced to announce publicly that they were saints and not mere sorcerers. However, because they announced their sainthood the Church condemned them for being prideful sorcerers.

The reason for such attitudes and practices of the Church was control. Magic was a form of control that the peasants possessed. As long as they had some control over themselves, the Church did not have total control over everything, which was what it was seeking. If the Church removed magic from the peasants, then the Church would have taken away control from the peasants, and it did. Without magic the peasants became totally dependant upon the Church for everything the practice of magic had once provided. They were forced to come to the Church and its associates, for healing and child birthing. They were forced to come to the Church for all of their spiritual and religious needs, now their contact with the divine was mediated, they had lost control over their spiritual lives as well as their daily lives.

Once the Church had all but stamped out the practice of magic among the peasants, it had complete control. Without anyone to teach the workings of magic to the next generations, the practice quickly became the stuff of superstition and legend. Magic, however, was not completely done away with in all forms. It still remained within the confines of the Church; there are nuances within the Orthodox Christian faith that qualify as acts of magic. The act of a priest calling upon God to bless a person is by definition an act of magic. The transubstantiation of the Eucharist is also an instance of magic at work within the Church.

With examples such as exorcism and blessings it can be said that magic has not left the world. The way in which people look at it is what has changed. Our modern western view of reality is narrow indeed, for we do not accept the existence of magic even though it is employed right in front of us on a regular basis. The Eucharist, though

Medieval Magick 47

it has the appearance and make-up of bread and wine, is the real presence of Christ transubstantiated by magic fueled by the power of God. We still believe in paradoxes, we still believe in magic, it is only our perceptions of such things that have changed. Reality is still the vast and mysterious realm it always has been, whether we acknowledge it or not.

The Flagellant Processions

This section has been included to teach only one thing: Mastery of the body, and thus both the transcendence from it and the abuse of it, is a powerful force. One may at times be tempted to use this power publicly, and while there are short-term positive results from spectacle, long-term negative results are possible. There is wisdom in secrecy and longevity in discretion.

> *"shut himself up in his cell and stripped himself naked and took his scourge with the sharp spikes, and beat himself on the body and on the arms and on the legs, till blood poured off him as from a man who has been cupped. One of the spikes on the scourge was bent crooked, like a hook, and whatever flesh it caught it tore off. He beat himself so hard that the scourge broke into three bits and the points flew against the wall. He stood there bleeding and gazed at himself. It was such a wretched sight that he was reminded in many ways of the appearance of the beloved Christ, when he was fearfully beaten. Out of pity for himself he began to weep bitterly. And he knelt down, naked and covered in blood, in the frosty air, and prayed to God to wipe out his sins from before his gentle eyes."*
>
> —Cohn (127)

In the overcrowded and desolate cities and towns of medieval Italy a movement began, the flagellant procession. The movement had its foundations with a hermit of the city of Perugia in the year 1260, and the movement quickly spread south towards Rome and north towards Lombard. From that year on, until the late 1400's the flagellant movement was a powerful force in medieval Europe.

The Flagellant Processions   49

The flagellant processions of the medieval times were both frightening and inspirational. In essence, the flagellants were punishers of their own bodies. They would pierce, flog, and beat themselves both in public and in private. This was all done with the hope of convincing God to have mercy upon the people, and visit them with less suffering and death. They hoped that because of their acts of self-torture God would forgive them of their sins, gift them with salvation, and make the world that they presently lived in a somewhat better place.

The tortures that they inflicted against themselves were almost inhuman. Many flogged themselves with a type of whip called a scourge; it consisted of a handle with several leather strips hanging off of it. Each one of these leather strips had a twisted piece of metal fastened to the end of it so that when a person was struck the bits of metal would tear out flesh with each strike. Other punishments involved torturing each other with hot iron spikes, simply burning and piercing the flesh until the person collapsed. Some even carried life-sized crucifixes upon their backs, punishing themselves by carrying the heavy structure over the many hard miles that the processions covered on their journeys. Some simply tied themselves up with rope and had themselves beaten, or they would just beat themselves.

The processions moved about from city to city, resting where they could and publicly torturing themselves. They were usually led by priests who had either given up on the church or had been forcibly removed from the church by their superiors. When the hordes of man and boys would arrive in a city they would march into the city bearing banners and burning candles. Once inside the city they would divide into groups and spread about the city, usually in front of local churches, and publicly punish themselves for hours at a time.

This public display of penance did a great deal to effect the masses that gathered to watch the flagellants. People began to put aside their differences with each other, criminals confessed their crimes and made amends, ursurs gave back ill gotten funds, and enemies became friends and many blood feuds were called off. As the processions moved on to the next town oftentimes a large number of people from each successive town would join the movement.

The flagellant processions had become a beacon of hope to the downtrodden and suffering masses of Europe. Soon the flagellants, as well as many of those who witnessed them, began to see themselves as not just working to absolve their own sins, but also the sins of others. Many of the flagellants believed that they were taking on the sins of the world and like Jesus were sacrificing their own bodies in order to save humankind. It was because of this that they were so accepted and loved by the masses of the towns and cities that they entered. They were given food, financial assistance, and always gained new members when they left.

In order to understand why these horrific processions were so successful one must look at the world in which they lived. Most of Europe's common people lived in harsh poverty. They were poorly clothed, starving, and constantly oppressed and harassed by the feudal state in which they lived. The Lords of the state demanded taxes and the Church demanded tithes, neither of which the peasants could pay and still be able to live and support their families. When wars would come the peasants had to support the armies that moved through the countries, and also suffered greatly when hostile forces would move upon their towns and villages. All to often the poor would be made to support one army, but not be given protection and then massacred by the next army.

The Church did little to help ease the suffering of the masses; in fact the Church was often seen as the enemy. Corrupt priests and clergy members took advantage of the laity as they disgraced women and burned "heretics", all the while demanding that each person pay tithes. The commoners could not see how going to church, receiving Holy Communion, and prayer were doing them any good. Loyalty to the Church seemed to have gotten them nowhere; it had even been harmful. Needless to say there was a great deal of rage and dissatisfaction

The Flagellant Processions   51

with the Church, and the flagellants offered another way for the masses to touch God.

Sometimes the flagellant processions would take a more revolutionary stance. When these revolutionary flagellants entered cities they looted and burned churches, killed and tortured priests, and preached against the Pope and the Church. These flagellants claimed that they could attain salvation through their own efforts and that they did not need the evil and corrupt Church to force them into anything.

It was during this time of revolutionary flagellants that the princes and bishops began to suppress the movements and burn some of the leaders as heretics. By the late 1200's there were two distinct groups of flagellants. The church and state generally tolerated the processions in Italy and France, because they were more orthodox in their theology and not revolutionaries. However, the processions in Germany were ever increasingly fanatical and revolutionary. Many of these flagellant movements were met with violence and condemnation as heretics.

A part of the reason for the German condemnation of some of the revolutionary flagellants as revolutionaries was because of the mystical significance of the number thirty-three and one half. In some of the earlier flagellant movements the processions lasted for thirty-three and one half days, the supposed number of years which were spent by Jesus Christ on earth. This mystical number, combined with the fact that many of the flagellant leaders of the time claimed to possess Heavenly Letters, divinely inspired words from God, gave the church and state amble grounds and reason to condemn and destroy many of the revolutionary flagellant processions from the late 1200's to the late 1300's.

The outbreak of the Black Plague served to ignite many more flagellant processions throughout Europe. If the poverty and oppression were not enough, the Black Death made matters even worse. Once again, like their predecessors in 1260, the new flagellants took up their scourges and began to march. Like before, the flagellant processions gave hope to the people and the movement grew in power and numbers.

The flagellant movement died out in the 1480's as the last of the flagellants either stopped marching or were burned as heretics. Other than the suppression of revolutionaries, the flagellant movements died out for one major reason, disillusionment. After decades of marching and penance the world just did not get any better for anyone. The plague continued, the poverty continued, the oppression and the corruption of the church continued. The flagellants, without their knowledge, began to unwittingly spread the very plague they were trying to stop. Without any advanced knowledge of disease control or sanitation, they carried the sickness with them everywhere they went. Once a member of the procession contracted the plague, the rest of the group was sure to get it and then spread it to whatever town they came in contact with. The very nature of the flagellant processions was perfect for the spread of the plague, with their constant beating and bleeding bodies. Many of the flagellant groups had also gotten wrapped up in eschatology and believed themselves to be living in the endtimes.

When the end never came, and they realized that what they were doing was not helping the situation, they could do nothing but lay down their scourges in defeat and go back home. They helped for a time, gave hope for a time, but in the end they could not make the changes they had sought to, a temporary solution to a very difficult and timeless situation.

The Little Apocalypse

Blood Magick is intensely personal and tremendously powerful, making such sorcerers key players in shaping the world. I may not be correct, but as the author will take what is my right, and say what I believe. In the following chapter I will use words like God, Good, and Evil. Please feel free to replace these words in your mind with any, more personally appropriate nomenclature should you feel so inclined.

Reality as a whole can exist in one of two ways, one is a state of harmonious discord and the second is disharmonious triviality. Harmonious discord is a state or condition of reality that is made possible by the constant struggle between stability and intensity. In this state Creation is at its best, it is wholly Good, this can be seen as the world as it should be. Ultimately, the world as God wants it to be, full of potentiality and a felt lure towards novelty.

Disharmonious triviality is the condition in which peace and stability exist but at the price of intensity. In this state of affairs the struggle of order and chaos has been stalled, there is no motion. Potentialities are denied, novelty never has the chance to occur because the lure toward creativity is no longer felt and \or responded too. This is the way God cannot possibly want the world to be, in this instance this would be wholly Evil.

In classical theology the eschaton, or for ease and clarity the apocalypse, is the triumph of Evil over Good for a time and finally the ultimate victor being the side of Good. This is a narrow view, in truth there is no end to Creation, the whole of reality is ever-unfolding, and so no ultimate end is conceived.

I think actual eschatology is made up of what will be called little apocalypses. These little apocalypses are temporary and small instances when portions of reality end up changing from harmonious discord to disharmonious triviality. It could be argued both ways as to whether the little apocalypses could become larger ones, thus making the disharmonious triviality more extensive and less temporary. One argument is that it would be impossible for the evil of disharmonious triviality to spread into the entirety of Creation. It could be argued that this would never happen because of the ever-present existence of potentialities and the creative impulse, that no matter what the potentialities would make their way into actuality and take hold. Also, my common assumption given my experience is that Creation is existent in ever unfolding infinity.

Another possible argument is that once the disharmonious triviality has taken hold that portion of reality becomes a source of more disharmonious triviality, and so it spreads. While for the sake of this text Creation is unarguably infinite, this disharmonious triviality could lockdown the potential in its area of influence. As this disharmonious triviality spreads more and more of Creation falls under its sway. Granted, creation is infinite, but the massive amounts of reality that are consumed would certainly give rise to the statement or observation that reality would be better off had that spread or occurrence of the disharmonious triviality not occurred. It is most arguably an apocalypse of Creation that would be better had is never come to pass.

Along with this approach comes an intrinsic element of Armageddon, the battle between good and evil. Classically good is seen as order and evil is seen as chaos, however, in this case I disagree. The components of harmonious discord is what is wholly Good in Creation, then both order and chaos can be seen as good. Necessary order can be perceived as good and chaos can be seen as necessary evil. Disharmonious triviality is the peace and stability bought at the price of intensity, and ultimately freedom.

The Little Apocalypse 55

What comes out of this battle between Good and Evil is an eschatology of the present. The apocalypse is now, in the dying of the present moment into the next, a little apocalypse, and Armageddon takes place at every transition. What is left is the individual. It is up to each individual actual entity to take part in the eschaton of each moment. Be that actual entity one who acts in the name of order as a hero, or that actual entity act as a chaotic villain of necessity, something must be done. It is not important what side one chooses, it is that a side is chosen. There must be a struggle, it is this struggle that gives rise to the state in reality of harmonious discord, the balance that is achieved by the conflict between order and chaos. Disharmonious triviality is the lost Armageddon, it is the cessation of that struggle between order and chaos. Disharmonious triviality is the apocalypse of stagnation. In process eschatology it is the decay of Creation that is the end of days.

However, more than the planned eschaton of classical theology, the everyday apocalypse in process requires individual action, as discussed above, and an unrelenting faith in God. In classical philosophy one is told from the start that all is decided and that God and Good will triumph in the end. One must have faith in a God that does not propagate a decided end. There is the possibility that all may not turnout well, that God may not triumph and Good not be the dominant and final way of reality. One does not have any assurance, none of the comfort provided by a planned and determined and final outcome. There is no final victory for God and Good, one can only have hope that God and Good can prevail as often as possible. Faith is paramount, and requires much more participation on the part of the believer and individual.

The time is always now.

Omega

We study magic to gain power. If we are all honest with ourselves we will not deny this. Under the search for power falls knowledge. We are human and thirst for it. If we study magic for these reasons alone, we will never be fully living up to our rightful potential. The third tier is humility. When we realize and accept our place in Creation we are able to grow into and beyond it.

0-595-29839-7

Made in the USA
Lexington, KY
25 August 2013